Rescission

of Contract

Inclusive of instructions:
Attorney's private notes on "How to
Prepare Legal Forms & Agreements"

Disclaimer

Because of possible unanticipated changes in governing statutes and case law relating to application of any information contained in this book, the author, publisher, and any and all persons or entities involved in any way in the preparation, publication, sale, or distribution of this book disclaim all responsibility for the legal effects or consequences of any use or action taken in reliance upon information contained in this book. No representations, express or implied, are made or given regarding the legal outcome of the use of any material found in this book.

Table of Contents

How to Prepare Legal Forms & Agreements

When preparing a legal form or contract, you should always pay close attention to the proper description and statement of the parties. In addition, the "name(s)" of the person(s) or business entities, or in some instances "both" which are going to be part of the document.

This may seem rather like general information, but it's really important that you get the proper description (and, the statement) of the parties perfectly correct the very first time.

Consider this: you may not (in everyday speech) address somebody quite so formally in conversation or perhaps in a business letter.

This is usually the case if it is somebody you know really well. However, you should still insert in the legal document their "complete name" instead of just a "shortened version."

For instance, type and/or write "Dr Peter J. Jones" instead of typing "Pete Jones." In the unlikely event you find yourself involved in future litigation then having the correct (and, full) name of the parties in the contract is crucial!

Why the Right Usage of Names?

Another important reason for having the right usage of names in a contract is it clearly defines the parties in the agreement and the terms and conditions.

By taking the time to establish ALL information (and pertinent details correctly, you will have "peace-of-mind" because there can be NO question about the parties' intentions later. This is especially so whenever the particulars have been changed and/or forgotten. Do not hesitate to correctly identify both parties by the location of their residence as well. For example:

When preparing a legal form type "Dr Peter J. Jones" which clearly states the party is "Dr Peter J. Jones, with the "current residential address" of "505 Gaming Street, Los Vegas Nevada." It is absolutely vital that you get this part right. In the eyes of the law you must have the "full and proper names" of the parties in the contract.

When you're doing business with a corporation (that's registered and state incorporated) make sure that you ask for an "original copy" of the articles of incorporation to verify that you have the name(s) correctly. Why?

Because there are literally millions of registered corporations (*and,* one person enterprises) in the United States, and it's possible to insert the entirely incorrect name because of subtle "differences" in names which are very similar.

Why It Doesn't Take Much for
Any Savvy Attorney to Dispute Your Claim

In some cases, it may be ALMOST impossible to bring about a successful case say for a "breach of contract" because a knowledgeable lawyer representing the other party, claims you've actually been dealing with some other company. . . *and not that of his clients.*

For example, you may have entered into a contract for a specific service on behalf of your customer. Let's say the name is: ACE Fencing Supplies Inc. You may think that it's correct but the actual name on file with the State may be, ACE Fencing & Supplies Inc.

It's a subtle difference in some cases, but it's enough to lose your case in a court of law! This may not seem like a big difference to you but in a court of law the judge may have second thoughts about awarding you damages if the name of the other party is not exactly what is registered with the State.

The sad fact is: a customer who doesn't wish to pay you under the terms and conditions of your contract could also be ready to say: *"Listen, the agreement for supplies wasn't with me or my business, so I don't owe you a single cent."*

Why It Is Essential To Identify the State
Where the Company Is Registered

Another vital issue for you to consider (when preparing a legal form and contract) is you must properly identify the "State" of where the corporation (or business) is registered. You should clearly define in the contract the full name of the business and where its offices are located. Remember that the more precise you are in "identifying the parties" the better the chance of *avoiding* any legal problems especially if it ever winds-up in a court of law.

The Crucial 'Consideration'

You should thoroughly review any business form or legal contract that you're about to enter into. Why? Because you should be able to easily identify somewhere early in the legal contract a statement that both parties agree on a certain amount of money, goods, products or services, etc.

This is known as the "consideration." The notion of a "consideration" in a legal contract has a long history in the law courts of America.

A "Consideration" simply denotes something of value in the eyes of the law. An exchange of consideration: whether it's financial or something else of "Value" is vital for any contract to be legally enforceable. Both of the parties who duly date and sign a contract must "give and receive" something of real value in the eyes of the law.

That "something of value" could be either that one party hand's over that they'd not otherwise be indebted to hand over or it could be "some right" that they give up that they'd otherwise have been entitled to exercise.

For example, if you agree to buy a car for cash then you must agree to "hand over" the cash directly to the seller, and the seller agrees to "hand over" the car to you. By doing so, you are providing a "consideration". Or the consideration could be something else of sufficient monetary value for the contract to be enforceable.

Other Types of "Consideration"

Here is an example of a totally different type of "Consideration". It is a "mutual release of claims" Let us say that you damage a parked automobile (by accident) and you offer to pay the owner $1,550 to settle out of court. In a case like this, you agree to "hand over" the $1,550 to the owner, and the owner agrees that he or she will not issue you with a summons. However, you MUST get the owner to sign a written "release of liability" or a "general release form" to prove you've settled this matter between both parties mutually.

Even though the owner did not give up anything physical, there is "consideration" to support the contract because the owner relinquished a legal right.

Term and Termination
A Powerful Contract Clause

Term and Termination: A powerful legal clause you should always insert in a contract is a "Term and Termination" provision. A legal agreement in most cases runs for a specific term or time period, and that period should be identified in the contract. The term may be stated in a simple wording as: *"The term of this Contract will be for 24-months as of the signing of this Contract"*

But what happens once the contract term has expired? You might think that the contract is finalised (*and,* usually it is) but in some circumstances (*and,* in some states of America) a legal contract may be deemed to automatically "renew" itself for an extended period of time and in most cases its equal to the initial term.

This could be true if the parties continue to "act" once the term has expired. However, this is NOT usually the case where it involves any business transactions or dealings in property.

For example: if you were to continue selling a certain brand of product, the customer may agree to continue to pay for it in accord with the original terms in the contract. He or she may reach a conclusion that agreement "has been extended" and for this reason, it may be essential to *clearly* state if you do or dot not intend for the agreement to be renewed.

A common strategy in contract litigation is for a defendant to argue the contract they were asked to sign is far too ambiguous, and capable of being interpreted in many different ways and areas.

One of the reasons this can be an effective strategy is because most U.S. States of America abide by a ruling on the way that legal contracts are to be interpreted by the courts, and any ambiguities are to be resolved.

In other words, if you are the person who prepared the contract and a legal provision of the contract can be interpreted both in a way that is favorable and unfavorable to you then a court of law will, in most cases, take the interpretation that is favourable to you and make a judgment against you.

Defendants will often take the most clearly worded agreement imaginable and bend over backwards trying to argue that they should not be liable, because some legal provisions are ambiguous. Regrettably, oftentimes a court of law will buy these ridiculous arguments. One way to protect yourself against having ambiguities automatically resolved against you is to use an interpretation clause. Here's a typical example of an interpretation clause:

"Any rule of law or legal decision that would require interpretation of any ambiguities in this agreement against the party that has drafted it is not applicable and waived. The provisions of this Agreement shall be interpreted in a reasonable manner to affect the purpose, sum and substance of the Agreement."

OR

"This Agreement will in all events be construed as a whole, according to its fair meaning, and not strictly for or against a party merely because that party (or the party's legal counsel) drafted the Agreement. The headings, captions, and titles in this legal Agreement are merely for reference and do not define, limit, extend, or describe the scope of this Agreement or any provision herein. Unless the context requires otherwise, (a) the gender

(Or lack of gender) of all words used in this Agreement includes the masculine, feminine, and neuter, and (b) the word including means including without limitation.

Amendment Clause

One of the most overlooked yet crucial provisions you can have in a contract is an "amendment clause." You should always include an amendment clause in any legal contract that you intend to date and sign.

Why?

Because, if it's not in the contract you run the real risk of winding-up with a contract that's not worth the paper it's written on. An amendment clause gives you a real edge over the other party because there's little the other party can legally do to weasel their way out of the agreed terms and conditions of the contract.

An example of a simple amendment clause is:

"Any modification of this Agreement will be effective only if it is in writing and signed by an authorised representative of each party of this agreement."

Another legal clause you need to have in a legal contract is an entirety clause or "zipper" clause as it's sometimes called. An entirety clause infers that the entire agreement between the parties is contained in the written contract.

Entire Agreement

It basically spells out that there are no other terms, agreements, representations or warranties other than those in the agreement. Just like an amendment clauses, this type of clause provides you with legal protection.

However, it's essential that ALL of the terms of the contract are clearly outlined in the contract otherwise you run the risk of it back firing on you if it ever gets to the point of litigation. An example clause:

"This legal Agreement contains the entire understanding between the parties. Each party to this agreement acknowledges that no other agreement, promise or statement contained in this Agreement shall be valid or binding."

OR

"This Agreement constitutes the entire agreement of the parties relating to the subject matter addressed in this Agreement. This Agreement supersedes all prior communications, contracts, or agreements between the parties with respect to the subject matter covered in this Agreement, whether oral or written"

Legal Warranties

The dos and don'ts of warranties and can they be avoided? Express warranties are avoided simply by not making any oral or written statements that could be considered a warranty.

In contrast, implied warranties by law must be expressly disclaimed. Almost everyone disclaims implied warranties, or at the very least, tries to. Sometimes the disclaimers are effective, but often times they are not especially if the matter goes before a local court of law.

The purpose of a disclaimer is to make sure that it is understood that the warranty, especially the ones implied, are not part of the deal. In a warranty disclaimer, you typically do two things:

(1) State that there are no express warranties being constructed other than those specifically stated in the contract, if any, and (2) state that there are no implied warranties being constructed, that the seller disclaims them, and the buyer is aware of it.

By law, buyers have to see the disclaimer for it to be effective. They also have to agree to it before they buy the product or service. That's why the limited warranty cards that are often placed in the box (or packaging) you buy are meaningless, because there's no opportunity for the buyer to read them before purchasing the goods.

In some States of America for example, they require warranty "disclaimers" to be clearly visible, in capital letters and in bold face print. A paragraph heading that clearly says "DISCLAIMER" is a good idea, too.

You will notice a sample warranty disclaimer is provided below, however, please note that your state may require extra language in order for the disclaimer to be legally valid. In addition, state law may not permit disclaimers in all cases.

Here is an example clause:

"DISCLAIMER [your business's name] MAKES NO WARRANTIES, EXPRESS OR IMPLIED, INCLUDING THE WARRANTIES OF GOOD AND WORKMANLIKE MANNER WITH RESEPECT TO ANY SERVICES PROVIDED, AND OF MERCHANTABILITY AND FITNESS WITH RESPECT TO ANY GOODS OR MATERIALS PROVIDED [your business's name], AND SHALL IN NO EVENT BE LIABLE FOR ANY DAMAGES INCLUDING CONSEQUENTIAL DAMAGES CLAIMED BY CUSTOMER".

Posted or "printed matter" disclaimers can reduce your liability exposure by telling readers and customers that they do business with you or use your information at their own risk.

The clauses can provide you with a legal defence if a patron tries to sue you for harm caused by your product or service. Some service companies use disclaimers to reduce expense risks, such as car rental contracts that usually offer customers the opportunity to buy extra collision insurance with the disclaimer that the agency will not be responsible for collision damage unless they do so.

Retailers can reduce their responsibility for product repairs by placing statements such as: *"There are no warranties, expressed or implied, other than those set forth in this contract"* on their sales documents. Businesses large and small can use disclaimers to set customer expectations at an acceptable level. It's far better to be up front with people these days by prominently posting a store's refund policy in direct view of the customer like at the cash register, etc. This also puts you in good standing with the law.

Deciding where to place disclaimers depends on the nature of your business. Typically, businesses include them in contracts; purchases orders and claims checks or hang signs inside the property.

For example, parking garages should post disclaimers on tickets or on signs. "Dry cleaners may have a disclaimer on their walls," or a retail store may post its return policy on the wall or on its credit card receipts." These days one of the most vital places to have a clearly marked and easily readable disclaimer is on your website. For example:

"THE MATERIALS ON THIS WEBSITE ARE PROVIDED "AS IS" WITHOUT ANY EXPRESS OR IMPLIED WARRANTY OF ANY KIND INCLUDING WARRANTIES OF MERCHANT-ABILITY, NONBREACH OF INTELLECTUAL PROPERTY OR FITNESS FOR A PARTICULAR PURPOSE. SITE OWNER OFFERS NO ASSURANCE OF UNINTERRUPTED OR ERROR FREE SERVICE. SITE OWNER DOES NOT WARRANT THE ACCURACY OR BROADNESSOF THE INFORMATION, TEXT, GRAPHICS, LINKS OR OTHER ITEMS CONTAINED ON THIS WEB SITE. SITE OWNER MAY CHANGE ANY

OF THE INFORMATION FOUND AT THIS SITE AT ANY TIME WITHOUTNOTICE INCLUDING THE TERMS OF SERVICE WITHOUT NOTICE. SITE OWNER MAKES NO COMMITMENT TO UPDATE THE INFORMATION FOUND AT THIS SITE. IN NO EVENT SITE OWNER BE LIABLE FOR ANY DAMAGES WHATSOEVERWITH, WITHOUT LIMITATION, DAMAGES FOR LOSS OF PROFITS, BUSINESS INTER-RUPTION, LOSS OF INFORMATION) ARISING OUT OF THE USE OR INABILITY TO USE THE MATERIAL OR INFORMATION AVAILABLE ON THIS SITE, EVEN IF SITE OWNER HAS BEEN ADVISED OF SUCH DAMAGES.

If you don't communicate this to the consumer you can easily invalidate your disclaimers. However, the above limitations may not apply in some cases.

Areas of Employment

Another area crucial area of concern when either drafting or entering into a legal contract is in the area of employment.

For example: A corporation sends one of their employees to a seminar so that the employee obtains additional skills and adequate qualifications.

However, oftentimes once an employee has advanced his or her level of skill they leave and find employment somewhere else for more money using their newfound skills and knowledge.

By using a legal clause in the employment contract you can in most cases prevent this from happening or at the very least slow it down significantly.

To do this you must insert in your employment contract a legal provision requiring repayment of any training expenses while the employee is under your employ. The legal clause should state that in the event the employee leaves after six months of employment, 100% of the training costs will be repaid. But if the employee leaves after twelve months 75% of the training costs will be repaid, and so on.

What's best about using this type of legal clause is that the employee is responsible and legally obligated to repay the training cost on the date of termination. In some instances, the employee is provided the option of signing a promissory note for the total training cost. Here is a typical employment clause that covers the cost of training employees:

"The employee realises and agrees that if he/she voluntarily terminates his/her employment with the Company, or is terminated for "Good Cause" as herein defined, the Employee shall reimburse the Company for the total amount of such tuition and travel-related expenses, depending on the length of the Employee's employment by the Company as of the date of termination, as follows:

1 - 12 months .... 75% reimbursement
13 - 18 months................. 50% reimbursement
19 -24 months .... 25% reimbursement
More than 24 months .... 0% reimbursement"

Non-Solicitation Provision

Another equally as important clause to use in an employment contract is a provision whereby you stop other corporations or businesses from poaching your best employees.

This is called a non-solicitation clause which prevents your customers from stealing your employees. It simply states that the customer will not solicit the employment of your employees during the time that you are offering a service to the customer. Or, it can include added time period usually up to 1-year. Here is a typical example of a non-solicitation clause:

"Customer shall not directly or indirectly solicit the employment of any _____ [company name] employee, and shall not employ any [company name] employee or any person who was an employee of [company name] at any time during the performance of the Services, for a period of one (1) year following the completion of the Services and any future services, sales, installation or other business arrangement by and between the parties concerned. In the unlikely event the Customer breaches the terms and conditions of this section, Customer shall pay _____ [company name] the sum of $_____ for each such breach".

Advice of Legal Counsel

Another area that is raised to the enforcement of a contract is that one party did not fully understand the terms of the contract or did not have the advice of a lawyer before the legal contract was signed.

This can happen when one party engaged the services of an attorney but the other party did not engage an attorney. To cover this issue and to prevent this from occurring is to use a clause in the contract which states that each party fully understands the agreement and has sought legal advice or at the very least has had the opportunity to seek legal counsel regarding the effect of the legal contract. A good example of an "Advice of Legal Counsel" clause is:

Each individual party to this Agreement represents and warrants to each other party that such party has read and fully understands the terms and provisions hereof, and has had an opportunity to review this Agreement with legal counsel, and has executed this Agreement based upon such party's own personal judgment and advice of independent legal counsel (if sought after).

Further Assurances Provision

Along with using an "Advice of Legal Counsel" clause it's also a savvy idea when entering into a contract where additional paperwork or filings will need to be completed after the contract is signed, that you include a "further assurances" clause, like the one below:

"In connection with this Agreement and the transactions contemplated hereby, each party to this Agreement will execute and deliver any additional documents and perform any extra acts that may be necessary or appropriate to effectuate and perform its obligations under this Agreement and the transactions contemplated hereby"

If you're about to enter into a contract and you are doubtful that a provision in the contract may be illegal or unenforceable under any applicable law you should insist on an "Invalid Provisions Clause" be inserted in the contract.

Non-Compete Provision

If you still have doubts as to whether a particular provision may exceed the limitations of applicable law (such as the term or geographic boundary of a non-compete provision in say an employment or franchise agreement) you should also add a "severance" or "invalid provisions" clause in the contract as well. Below is a general example:

"If any provision of this Agreement is held to be illegal, invalid, or unenforceable under any present or future law, then that provision will be fully severable. This Agreement will be construed and enforced as if the illegal, invalid, or unenforceable provision had never comprised a part of this Agreement, and the remaining provisions of this Agreement will remain in full force and effect and will not be affected by the illegal, invalid, or unenforceable provision or by its severance from this Agreement. Furthermore, in lieu of each such illegal, invalid, or unenforceable provision, there will be added automatically, as a part of this Agreement, a provision as similar in terms to such illegal, invalid, or unenforceable provision as may be possible and be legal, valid and enforceable"

Now, when it comes to signing a contract make sure that the contract is endorsed and countersigned. The requirements for endorsement vary considerably from state to state so it's best to first consult with an attorney and find out the legal requirements which meet State and federal law. Generally, endorsement is usually required when dealing with wills, realty documents, or other documents that may need to be filed in the public records.

It's vital to have a document endorsed especially if there is any concern that the person signing the agreement may later deny the authenticity of his or her signature on the documents. The type of endorsement can differ from state to state, so again you should seek the advice of an attorney in this matter. Listed below are the types of endorsement for both a person and for the endorsement of an individual signing in their capacity as an officer of a corporation. Sample endorsement for an individual:

COUNTY OF _____ §
COUNTY OF _____ §

Before me, the undersigned authority, on this day personally appeared {name}, known to me to be the person whose name is subscribed to the foregoing instrument, and upon his {her}oath acknowledged to me that he {she} executed the same for the purposes and consideration therein expressed.

SWORN TO AND SUBSCRIBED BEFORE ME THIS _____ DAY OF _____, 20 ___.

NOTARY PUBLIC
My Commission Expires: _____.

Example endorsement for a corporation or separate entity:

COUNTY OF _____ §
COUNTY OF _____ §

Before me, the undersigned authority, on this day personally appeared {name}, the {title}of {entity}, known to me to be the person whose name is subscribed to the foregoing instrument, and upon his {her} oath acknowledged to me that he {she} executed the same for the purposes and consideration therein expressed and in the capacity therein stated.

SWORN TO AND SUBSCRIBED BEFORE ME THIS _____ DAY OF _____, 20 ___.

NOTARY PUBLIC
My Commission Expires: _____.

The Difference between a Contract and Agreement

A contract is written. It typically makes an offer to buy, sell or offer services, and the second party offers binding payment. A contract is legally binding if drafted strongly and duly dated and signed by both parties. In the eyes of the law, a contract requires it to be witnessed by legally appropriate witnesses.

An agreement is usually verbal and unless both parties can show evidence in a court of law that they agreed to the stated terms set forth, and in front of a judge, it is extremely difficult to enforce in a legal and binding manner. The law defines a contract as every agreement and promise which is enforceable by law. According to Section #2b of the Contract Act, an agreement enforceable by law is a contract. A contract must contain two essential elements: (1) An agreement and (2) the agreement should be enforceable by law.

Alphabetical List of Legal Clauses

Acceleration

(Clause for acceleration on default of payment)

Acceleration on Default: If _____ should fail to pay any instalment at the time the same becomes due under the terms of this Agreement, or to pay interest when due, the entire sum payable under this Agreement shall immediately become due and payable.

Access to Information

(Agreement clause that can be inserted in a contract, which provides a [party], access to confidential information with respect to the contract)

Access to Information: The Undersigned in the course of examining the Company's records and business will have access to or learn certain information belonging to the Company that is proprietary and confidential.

Access to Records

(Agreement clause, which can be inserted into a manufacturing agreement, which provides the customer access to manufacturer's accounting records with respect to the contract)

Access to Records: The Manufacturer shall maintain complete and accurate accounting records in accordance with generally accepted accounting principles, with respect to all aspects of the manufacture, supply and delivery of the [products], and shall retain such records for a period of _____ year(s) from the date of receipt of final payment from the Customer. In the event that the Customer requests an audit of such accounting records, the Manufacturer shall allow the auditors access to all such accounting records and shall cooperate fully with the auditors in order to enable them to conduct such audit.

Agreement Binding

(Clause stating the binding legal obligations upon the parties and their heirs)

Agreement Binding: This Agreement is binding upon and inures to the benefit of the parties hereto, their heirs, administrators, executors, and assigns.

Agreement to Transfer Title of Ownership [Real Estate Agreement]

(Clause stating Transferor's right, title and interest, in Real Estate property)

Transferor will transfer all the land, with the buildings

and improvements on the land, being in the [description of property]. This transfer of property includes all of Transferor's right, title, and interest, in and to any land in the bed of any street, road, or avenue opened or proposed, in front of or adjoining the premises, to the centre line, and all of Transferor's right, title, and interest in and to any award made or to be made in lieu of Transferor's right, title, and interest in and to any unpaid award for damage to the premises by reason of change of grade of any street; and Transferor will execute and deliver to Transferee, on closing of title, or thereafter on demand, all instruments reasonably needed for the conveyance and the assignment and collection of any award.

Air-Conditioning and Heating [Commercial Lease Agreement]

(Agreement clause for additional provisions in a commercial property lease agreement)

Prior to taking possession of the premises, Tenant shall take whatever steps Tenant deems necessary to satisfy Tenant that the commercial air-conditioning, heating equipment, cooling systems, and mechanical equipment as installed by Landlord are in accordance with the plans and specifications, and that the installation is satisfactory and acceptable to Tenant. Upon occupancy of the premises and acceptance of the air-conditioning, heating and cooling systems, and installations, Tenant shall assume full and complete responsibility for their operation, maintenance, repair, and replacement, except for the maintenance, repair, and replacement assumed by Landlord under Landlord's guarantee. Except as provided in Landlord's guarantee, Landlord shall not be liable to Tenant for the failure or discontinuance of the air-conditioning, heating, and cooling systems, or for the provision of any other utility service to the Demised Premises. Landlord shall assign to Tenant any and all warranties obtained by Landlord regarding such air-conditioning and heating systems, at the time of commencement of this lease.

Amendments

(Agreement clause providing a written legal provision for future amendments to a duly dated and signed agreement)

Amendments: This agreement may be amended at any time and from time to time, but any amendment must be in writing and signed by each person.

Arbitration

(Agreement clause for the appointment of arbitrators in the event of a dispute between the parties under the agreement)

Arbitration: All disputes between the parties in relation to this Agreement shall be referred to the arbitration of a single arbitrator, if the parties agree upon such arbitrator, otherwise to a panel of three (3) arbitrators, one (1) to be appointed by each of the parties, and a third to be chosen by the first two arbitrators so named. The award and determination of the arbitrator or arbitrators, or any two of the three arbitrators shall be binding upon the parties and their respective heirs, executors, administrators and assigns.

OR

All disputes arising in connection with this Agreement shall be settled under the Rules of Conciliation and Arbitration of the International Chamber of Commerce by one or more arbitrators appointed in accordance with the said Rules.

OR

Any disputes pertaining to the liquidation of the Partnership and the winding up of the Partnership's affairs that cannot be settled amicably between the Partners shall be submitted to an arbitrator under the Rules then obtaining of the American Council of Arbitration or like organization in the City of [city], whose award may be reduced to judgment in any court of competent jurisdiction.

Arbitration (Alternative)

(Alternative/Optional clause, which can be inserted into an agreement, providing for arbitration to be governed by the state of [State] this clause is for use in contracts, which will be governed by local shire law)

Any dispute or disagreement of any kind between the Buyer and the Seller this agreement shall be resolved by binding arbitration in accordance with the laws of the county of [County]

The arbitration tribunal shall consist of three (3) arbitrators chosen by the parties from a slate of eight (8) proposed arbitrators provided by the American Council of Arbitration or like Organization. If the parties are unable to agree on all three arbitrators within seven (7) days after receipt of the slate provided by the American Council of Arbitration or like Organization, the American Council of Arbitration or like organization shall appoint the number of arbitrators the parties have been unable to agree upon from the slate. The decision of the tribunal shall be final and binding and no appeal shall lie there from. The tribunal shall have the power to order one party to contribute to the reasonable costs and expenses of the other party, or to pay all or any portion of the costs of the arbitration, as the panel determines in its discretion.

Assignment [General]

(Agreement clause stating non-assignment of the agreement obligations by either party)

Assignment: This Agreement may not be assigned by either party without the prior written consent of the other. Undersigned [Name] may not delegate Undersigned's duties/responsibilities under this Agreement to another person or entity without [name] prior written consent.

Audit Services

(Agreement clause providing the avenue for Examining Company/Personal records, etc.)

Audit Services. We will examine the [name] (Company) balance sheet as of [date] and the related statements of income, retained earnings, shareholders' equity, and changes in financial position for the financial year then ended. Our examination will be made in accordance with generally accepted auditing standards and will include those tests of Company's accounting records and other procedures that we consider necessary to enable us to render an opinion on the fairness of Company's financial statements.

Board of Director's/Managers [Partnership Agreement]

(Clause which can be inserted into a partnership agreement, providing for the appointment of a board of Director's to manage the partnership business.)

Board of Director's/Managers: Unless otherwise determined by a special majority vote of two-thirds of all Partnership interests, the affairs of the Partnership shall be managed by a Board of Director's/Managers (the "Board") comprising such of the Partners as the Partners may from time to time determine; provided, however, that the Board shall have no authority to make any determination with respect to the interest of each Partner in the Partnership and the assets, profits and liabilities thereof nor to admit new Partners, nor shall the Board have any authority to enter into any contract or obligation which involves an expenditure in excess of $_____ without the prior written approval of the Partners. The Board shall consult with the Partners as they see fit on management of the affairs of the

Partnership and may call general meetings of the Partnership to obtain the advice and direction of the other Partners. The Board shall be authorised to take such steps as may be required to carry out its decisions; provided, however, with respect to any substantial matters, the Board shall keep minutes which shall be circulated to the other Partners and any one of the Partners shall be entitled to call, within [--] days of receipt of a copy of such minutes, a general meeting of the Partnership to consider any decision taken by the Board. The Board shall meet at such times and shall conduct its affairs as it shall see fit and a majority of the members of the Board shall constitute a quorum. All decisions of the Board made at any such meeting shall be made by simple majority vote among the members present at the meeting.

Cancellation of Purchase Order [Manufacturing Agreement]

(Agreement clause which, can be inserted into a manufacturing agreement, setting out the conditions under which customer has the right to cancel a purchase order.)

MANUFACTURING AGREEMENT
Cancellation of Purchase Order clauses: The Customer shall have the right to cancel any purchase order by giving notice to the Manufacturer in writing at least days/weeks prior to the date of delivery. The Customer shall pay the Manufacturer for all work in progress at the time of such cancellation, upon delivery of the same to the Customer, and the Customer's liability shall be strictly limited to such work in progress.

If the Manufacturer shall be unable to fill any portion of a purchase order within (days/weeks/months) of the delivery date stated in such purchase order, the Customer shall have the right to cancel such purchase order, and shall not be liable for any costs or damages to the Manufacturer with respect to any work completed or in progress under such purchase order.

Caveats and Liens [Construction Contract]

(Agreement clause which can be inserted into a building agreement (construction contract) dealing with lien holdbacks, waiver of lien, performance bonds, indemnification, and bankruptcy of the general contractor.)

Waiver: The Contractor hereby renounces and waives any right to any caveat or lien for work completed or to be completed, services rendered or to be rendered, or materials furnished or to be furnished, with respect to the Building, and any right to register a lien claim against the Building or the lands upon which the Building is situate.

Construction Financing [Construction Contract]

(Clause which can be inserted into a construction contract providing for construction mortgage advances, lien holdbacks and default by the borrower.)

Advances at Lender's Discretion: The Lender shall make such advances under the Mortgage at such times and in such sums as it may deem proper and prudent having regard to the progress of the work and the value from time to time of the Project, and the cost of completion of the Project. The Lender shall not be required to advance the full amount under the Mortgage unless, in the opinion of the Lender, the value of the Project shall be of the full value of the Mortgage. For this purpose, the Lender shall have the right to have the Project inspected by an inspector or valuator to determine the value of the Project at any given time. All fees charged by such inspector or valuator shall be payable by the Borrower and shall form part of the indebtedness of the Borrower to the Lender, and shall bear interest at the same rate at the mortgage rate.

Construction Insurance [Construction Contract]

(Agreement clause which can be inserted into a binding building agreement or construction contract, dealing with insurance of "damage to" and "destruction of" the building during construction.)

(a) Damage to Work in Progress. All work on the Building shall be done at the risk of the Contractor until the Building is completed, and the costs of any damage to the work on the Building prior to completion shall be borne by the Contractor.

(b) Destruction of Building. If prior to completion, the Building and the work in progress should be totally destroyed by fire, accident or other acts of God which the Contractor could not have reasonably foreseen, the portion of the loss occasioned by such destruction which is to be borne by the Owner shall not exceed the total amounts due under this Agreement, and any balance shall be borne by the Contractor. (c) Insurance. The Owner shall insure to its full insurable value the Building, materials and supplies jointly in the names of the Owner and the Contractor against loss or damage by fire, with loss payable to the Owner and the Contractor as their respective interests may appear, and the costs of such insurance shall be borne by the Contractor.

Commercial Project [Building Contract]

(A variety of miscellaneous clauses, which can be inserted into a building agreement, dealing with: on-site control by the engineer, hiring a site foreman, security, conduct of employees, loss or damage to work, provision of utilities and services, delivery and storage of materials, clean-up of work-site.)

Work Subject to Control of Engineer. The work performed shall in every respect be under and subject to the control and supervision of the Engineer, and all orders, directions or instructions given by the Engineer to the Contractor with respect to any aspect of the work performed shall be promptly and efficiently be performed and complied with, to the Engineer's specifications.

Foreman: A competent foreman shall be employed by the Contractor and present at the Site during all working hours, and shall take orders and instructions from the Engineer. Such foreman shall be considered the lawful representative of the Contractor, and shall have full power to carry out all orders, directions and instructions of the Engineer, but this clause shall not relieve the Contractor from its duties hereunder.

Security: The Contractor is to employ at all times outside of regular working hours a security guard to oversee the worksite until the Project is completed.

Competing Business [Partnership Agreement]

(Clause which can be inserted in a partnership agreement setting out provisions for allowing or restricting a partners' interest in a competing businesses)

Right to Compete with Partnership Business: The Partners shall have directly or indirectly, any trade or business other than the business of the Partnership, including any trade or business that competes with the business of the Partnership.

Accounting of Outside Income: No Partner shall be liable to account to the other Partners for any income earned outside of the business of the Partnership except for any income earned from a business that competes with the business of the Partnership, or from undisclosed transactions involving the use of the Partnership name, property or business connections.

Compliance with Federal Law [Sale Agreement]

(Agreement clause providing guarantee of delivery of [Goods and/ or Property] in accord with the terms and conditions of a sale agreement)

Compliance with Federal Law: In compliance with

Federal law of [state], Seller shall prepare and deliver to Buyer, no later than [number] days before the closing, a list of Seller's creditors. The list shall be signed and sworn to or affirmed by Seller or Seller's agent. The list shall contain the names and business addresses of all of Seller's creditors, the amounts owed to them, if known, and the names and business addresses of all parties known by Seller to assert claims against Seller even if the claims are disputed. In addition, Seller will give Buyer a list of the business names and business addresses used by Seller during the three years ending with the date of this Agreement.

Condition Precedent

(Clause setting out condition(s) to be met prior to coming into effect, failing which the agreement is void.)

Condition Precedent: This Agreement is executed subject to the following condition(s):

On performance of the condition(s), this Agreement shall be in force and binding upon the parties, but otherwise it shall be void. This condition is inserted for the benefit of _____ and may be waived at its option; upon waiver of the condition, this Agreement shall be in force and binding upon the parties.

Confidentiality

(Agreement clause which can be inserted into a legal agreement, dealing with confidentiality between the parties to the agreement)

Confidentiality: Each of the parties hereto agrees to keep confidential and not to disclose, directly or indirectly, any information regarding the other party's business, including without limitation, information with respect to operations, procedures, methods, accounting, technical data or existing or potential customers, or any other information which the other party has designated as confidential.

PARTY1 agrees that PARTY1, its employees, agents and representatives shall not, either during the term of this Agreement or at any time thereafter, disclose any proprietary, secret or confidential information of PARTY2 to any third party whatsoever without the express written consent of PARTY2.

PARTY1 shall secure all documents work in process, products or other items incorporating any of the Confidential Information in locked file drawers or areas to which access is restricted in order to prevent its unauthorised disclosure. Neither party to this Agreement shall disclose the existence of this Agreement in any communication, written or verbal, to any third party without the prior written consent of the other party.

Compensation

(Agreement clause providing an itemised account for compensation as outlined in a signed agreement.)

Compensation: Our fee for these services is........ Dollars ($........), payable........ Dollars ($........) on your signing this agreement......... Dollars ($........) of weeks [number] thereafter, and the balance upon the completion of our engagement.

OR

Compensation: Our fee for these services will be computed at our standard per diem rates, which are [description], which, together with any out-of-pocket costs, will be billed to you every [number] weeks as the work progresses. All invoices are payable when rendered.

OR

Compensation: Client will pay Consultant a consulting fee of .... dollars ($........) per day (minimum of eight hours and prorated for partial days) for work performed by Consultant under this Agreement. The consulting fee shall be payable at the end of each month in which Consultant furnishes services pursuant to this Agreement.

[Alternative Paragraph]

Compensation: Client agrees to pay Consultant a consulting fee of........ dollars ($........) per hour for work performed by Consultant under this Agreement. Consultant will invoice Client at the end of each month for consulting fees due with respect to work performed by Consultant under this Agreement during that month, with payment due within [number] days after receipt of each invoice.

Consultant an Independent Contractor

(Clause providing an outline of specific services by a consultant as an independent contractor)

Consultant an Independent Contractor: Consultant will furnish Consultant's services as an independent contractor and not as an employee of Client or of any company affiliated with Client. Consultant has no power or authority to act for, represent, or bind Client or any company affiliated with Client in any manner. Consultant is not entitled to any medical coverage, life insurance, participation in Client's savings plan, or other benefits afforded to Client's regular employees, or those of Client's affiliated companies. If Client or any of Client's affiliated companies is required to pay or withhold any taxes or make any other payment with respect to fees payable to Consultant, Consultant will reimburse Client or the company in full for taxes paid, and permit Client to make deductions for taxes required to be withheld from any sum due Consultant.

Consultant Not to Engage in Conflicting Activities

(Agreement clause providing client with a promise of exclusivity to consulting services)

Consultant Not to Engage in Conflicting Activities: During the time of this Agreement, Consultant will not enter into any activity, employment, or business arrangement that conflicts with Client's interests or Consultant's obligations under this Agreement. In view of the sensitive nature of Consultant's status, Client shall have the option of terminating this Agreement at any time if, in Client's sole judgment, a conflict of interest exists or is imminent. Consultant will advise Client of Consultant's position with respect to any activity, employment, or business arrangement contemplated by Consultant that may be relevant to this Paragraph. For this purpose, Consultant agrees to disclose any such plans to Client prior to implementation.

Contribution of Additional Capital [Partnership Agreement]

(Clause which can be inserted into a partnership agreement, providing for contribution of additional funds from partners when necessary to top up operating capital)

Contribution of Additional Capital: If at any time the value of the net assets of the Partnership shall descend below $_____, the Partners shall contribute such further amounts of capital in proportion to their interests in the Partnership as are necessary to increase the value of the net assets to $_____ or such other value as the Partners may deem necessary. If any Partner shall be unable to make such further contribution, the remaining Partners may either contribute to capital, if all Partners consent to such contribution, in which event the interest of each Partner shall be re-apportioned to reflect his total capital contribution, or may lend sufficient monies to the Partnership, at such interest rate as may be agreed on, without affecting the interest of any Partner.

Correction to Existing Agreement

(Clause stating the intent of the agreement is to correct an error in an existing agreement.)

Correction of Existing Agreement: The intention of this Agreement is to correct an instrument executed by the parties dated the _____ day of _____, 20 __, and to express the true agreement between the parties as of that date.

Covenant Not to Sue

(Covenant not to sue given by one or more persons (covenantors) who may have an interest, right or claim arising under a particular agreement. Each of the covenantors covenants with the parties to the agreement that they will not sue any of them in respect to the agreement, and acknowledging what the extent of their interest is.)

COVENANT NOT TO SUE AND ACKNOWLEDGEMENT

Each of the undersigned, on behalf of itself or himself, as the case may be, and their respective successors, heirs, executors, administrators and assigns, for and in consideration of ONE DOLLAR ($1.00) and other good and valuable consideration, the receipt and sufficiency of which is hereby acknowledged by the undersigned, does hereby acknowledge, agree and covenant with PARTY1 and with PARTY2 that the undersigned will take no action whatsoever in any jurisdiction wheresoever and will not commence any proceedings againstPARTY1, PARTY2, or their respective directors, officers, employees, shareholders, heirs, executors, insurers, administrators, agents, professional or other advisors, or assigns, in relation to any matter arising out of the_____ dated _____ between_____ and _____ or in relation to any dealings whatsoever with PARTY3.

Damage and Insurance [Construction]

(Clauses which can be inserted into a building agreement or construction contract, dealing with insurance of, damage to and destruction of the building during construction)

Insurance: The Owner shall insure to its full insurable value the Building, materials and supplies jointly in the names of the Owner and the Contractor against loss or damage by fire, with loss payable to the Owner and the Contractor as their respective "interests" may appear, and the costs of such insurance shall be borne by the Contractor.

Damage to Work in Progress: All work on the Building shall be done at the risk of the Contractor until the Building is completed, and the costs of any damage to the work on the Building prior to completion shall be borne by the Contractor.

Destruction of Building: If prior to completion, the Building and the work in progress should be totally destroyed by fire, accident or other acts of God which the Contractor could not have reasonably foreseen, the portion of the loss occasioned by such destruction which is to be borne by the Owner shall not exceed the total amounts due under this Agreement, and any balance shall be borne by the Contractor.

Death of Partner [Partnership Agreement]

(Clause which can be inserted into a partnership agreement setting out options to the remaining partner if the other partner dies or becomes insolvent)

Death of a Partner: If either Partner should die or become insolvent, the other Partner, if mutually agreeable, shall remain in the Partnership with the estate of the deceased or insolvent Partner; provided that, if either party is not agreeable to remaining in the Partnership, then the remaining Partner may purchase the interest of the deceased or insolvent Partner from his estate. The purchase price for such purchase shall be as agreed on between the remaining Partner and the estate of the deceased or insolvent Partner. If the parties cannot reach an agreement, then the purchase price shall be set by arbitration in accordance with the provisions of Article _____. The remaining Partner shall be entitled to retain the name of the Partnership. If the remaining Partner does not desire to continue the Partnership and does not wish to purchase the interest of the deceased or insolvent Partner from his estate, then the business of the Partnership shall be sold and the surplus after payment of all debts and liabilities of the business shall be divided equally between the Partner and the estate of the deceased or insolvent Partner.

Defalcation, Fraud, or Irregularities

Defalcation, Fraud, or Irregularities: The Company does not expect to make a detailed examination of all your transactions nor do we expect that we will necessarily discover defalcations, fraud, or other irregularities, if they exist. The Company will inform you of any unusual or abnormal situation that we might discover.

Defective or Substandard Work or Materials

(Clause that can be inserted into a building contract which provide for authority given to the engineer to allow the engineer to deal with issues of defective work/ materials, shortages of materials or workmen)

Defective Work or Materials: If, in the Engineer's sole opinion, the Contractor shall use or employ, or intend to use or employ, any materials, plant, tools, equipment, parts, supplies, transport or any other thing whatsoever, which the Engineer finds are not in accordance with the provisions of this Agreement or are in any way unsuitable, substandard or undesirable for use in constructing the Project, or any part thereof, or should the Engineer consider that any work is, for any reason, insufficiently executed or performed, the Engineer may order the Contractor to remove the same, and to use and employ proper material, plant, tools, equipment, parts, supplies or other things as decided by the Engineer, or to properly re-execute and perform such work, as the case may be, and thereupon the Contractor shall immediately comply with such orders and if the

Contractor fails to comply with such orders within twenty-four (24) hours the Engineer may, at any time thereafter or cause to be executed the orders so given, and the Contractor shall, on demand, pay to the Owner all costs, damages and expenses incurred in respect thereof, or incurred by the Owner by reason of the Contractor's non-compliance with any such orders, or the Owner may, in its sole discretion, retain and deduct such costs, damages and expenses from any amounts then or thereafter payable to the Contractor.

Definition of Confidential Information

(Agreement clause providing access to proprietary information under certain terms and conditions)

Definition of Confidential Information: The term "Confidential Information," as used throughout this Agreement, means any secret or proprietary information relating directly to the Company's business and/or subsidiaries, including, but not limited to, products, customer lists, pricing policies, employment records and policies, operational methods, marketing plans and strategies, product development techniques or plans, business acquisition plans, new personnel acquisition plans, methods of manufacture, technical processes, designs and design projects, inventions and research programs, trade know-how, trade secrets, specific software, algorithms, computer processing systems, object and source codes, user manuals, systems documentation, and other business and financial affairs of the Company and affiliated companies and subsidiaries.

Delivery [Manufacturing Agreement]

(Agreement clause which can be inserted into a manufacturing agreement, setting out obligations of manufacturer for delivery under purchase orders, manufacturer's option to fill an order in instalments, force majeure clause relieving manufacturer of liability if circumstances do not permit delivery (acts of God, strikes, etc.)

MANUFACTURING AGREEMENT
Delivery of Products: The Manufacturer shall deliver the Products to the Customer in accordance with the instructions given on the purchase order on the date and to the place specified on the purchase order, or to such other place or on such other date as the parties may agree in writing.

OR

Delivery, Title, Risk of Loss and Inspection

(a) Manufacturer shall not be liable in any respect for failure to ship or for delay in shipment of products pursuant to accepted orders where such failure or delay shall have been due wholly or in part to shortage or curtailment of material, labour, transportation or utility services, or to any labour or production difficulty in manufacturers plants or those of its suppliers, or to any cause beyond manufacturers control or without manufacturers fault or negligence, and manufacturers shall not be liable for shipping products over routes or by means of transportation other than as specified by distributor.

(b) Title to and risk of loss of the product shall pass to distributor on manufacturers placing such Products in the custody of a carrier for shipment to distributor.

(c) Within _____ days following the date of receipt by distributor, distributor shall inspect the products and shall immediately notify manufacturer of any defects in the products.

(d) Failure by distributor to notify manufacturer in writing of any defects in the products within the _____ days shall be conclusive proof that the products have been received by distributor without defects. Manufacturer shall in no event have any responsibility for any damage caused to the Products during shipment. It shall be the sole responsibility of distributor to file any appropriate claims for reimbursement with the carrier.

Dispute Resolution Clause

(Optional clause, which can be inserted into an agreement, setting out a procedure for resolving disputes arising with respect to the agreement failing a resolution, the parties agree to go to arbitration. If this still fails to resolve the situation, the parties agree to go to court)

Dispute Resolution: The parties recognise that issues may arise between them which they disagree upon. The parties therefore agree that the following provisions shall apply to any disagreement or dispute between the parties in any way arising out of this agreement, the interpretation of this agreement, or the rights or obligations of the parties as follows: (a) If there is an issue or dispute between the parties which they cannot resolve between themselves, they shall work together in good faith for at least fourteen (21) days from the time the issue arises to try and resolve the differences in question before taking any further action under this agreement. (b) If the dispute is not resolved within fourteen days, their respective Director's will communicate directly with each other in an effort to resolve the parties' differences. (c) If the dispute is not resolved within a further fourteen (21) days, the parties agree to appoint and obtain the assistance of a mutually acceptable mediator to mediate their differences. (d) If the dispute is not resolved, or the parties cannot agree upon a mediator, within a further fourteen (21) days, then either party may initiate legal proceedings in the court of competent jurisdiction in the [County/State] of [--------].

Duration of Agreement

(Agreement clause providing secret and confidential information for the duration of a contractual arrangement)

Duration of Agreement: The obligations imposed on the Undersigned shall continue with respect to each unit of the Confidential Information, and such obligations shall not terminate until such unit shall cease to be secret and confidential and shall be in the public domain, unless such event shall have occurred as a result of wrongful conduct by the Undersigned or the Undersigned's agents, servants, officers, or employees or a breach of the covenants set forth in this Agreement.

Entire Understanding

(Agreement clause outlining the complete and entire understanding between the parties)

This Agreement contains the entire understanding between the parties and supersedes all previous agreements regarding termination and liquidation of the Partnership, whether oral or in writing. This Agreement cannot be modified or terminated except in accordance with its terms or by writing signed by both parties.

Entire Agreement and Modification: This Agreement contains the entire agreement between the parties. This Agreement may not be modified except by later written agreement signed by both parties.

OR

Entire Understanding: This Agreement sets forth the entire understanding between the parties with respect to the subject matter hereof and may not be modified, changed, or amended, except by writing signed by the party to be charged.

Equitable Relief

(Agreement clause providing Company rights and remedies under specific terms and conditions of the agreements)

Equitable Relief: The Undersigned acknowledges and agrees that a breach of the provisions of Paragraphs [--] or [--] of this Agreement would cause the Company to suffer irreparable damage that could not be adequately remedied by an action at law. Accordingly, the Undersigned agrees that the Company shall have the right to seek specific performance of the provisions of Paragraphs [--] and [--] to enjoin a breach or attempted breach of the provisions thereof, such right being in addition to all other rights and remedies that are available to Company at law, in equity, or otherwise.

Exercise of Option

(Agreement clause providing an exclusive right to exercise an option of purchase pursuant to the terms and conditions of an agreement)

Exercise of Option: Purchaser may exercise its exclusive right to purchase the Premises pursuant to the Option, at any time during the Option Term, by giving written notice thereof to Seller. As provided for above, the date of sending of said notice shall be the Option Exercise Date. In the event the Purchaser does not exercise its exclusive right to purchase the Premises granted by the Option during the Option Term, Seller shall be entitled to retain the Option Fee, and this agreement shall become absolutely null and void and neither party hereto shall have any other liability, obligation or duty herein under or pursuant to this Agreement.

Export Restrictions [Manufacturing]

(Agreement clause which can be inserted into a manufacturing agreement, setting out the export restrictions on technical information)

MANUFACTURING AGREEMENT

Export Restrictions: This Agreement and any confidential information provided by either party to the other hereunder is subject to any restrictions that may be imposed by the _____ Government concerning the export of technical information from _____.
Each party hereto covenants and agrees with the other that it shall not export, directly or indirectly, any confidential information acquired under this Agreement, or any Items utilizing any such confidential information to any country for which the _____ Government or any agency thereof requires an export license or other form of governmental approval, without first having obtained the written consent of the Department of _____ or other agency of the _____ Government when required to do so by applicable law.

Export Restrictions

(Agreement clause which can be inserted into an agreement, setting out restrictions on the export of confidential or proprietary information)

Export Restrictions. [Choose one of the following]
This agreement, and any confidential information provided under this agreement, is subject to any restrictions concerning the export of Products or technical information from _____ which may be imposed by the _____ Government.

Accordingly, each party agrees that it will not export, directly or indirectly, any confidential information acquired under this agreement or any Products utilising any such confidential information to any country for which the _____ Government or any agency thereof at the time of export requires an export licence or other governmental approval, without first obtaining the written consent to do so from the Department of _____ or other agency in the _____ Government when required by an applicable statute or regulation.

OR

The Buyer agrees that it will not knowingly export from _____, directly or indirectly, any technical information acquired from the Seller under this agreement or any Products utilising any such technical information.

Expulsion of Partner [Partnership Agreement]

(Agreement clause which can be inserted into a partnership agreement, setting out the terms under which a partner can be expelled from the partnership by the other partners)

Expulsion of Partner: If any Partner should become insolvent or bankrupt, or be convicted of any criminal offence, or perform any of the acts prohibited by this Agreement, such Partner may be expelled from the Partnership on unanimous vote of the remaining Partners, and his interest in the Partnership purchased by the remaining Partners. The purchase price of such interest shall be calculated as set out in the valuation procedure described in paragraph _____ and paid to the expelled Partner in equal _____ instalments over a period of _____ years, without interest. The expelled Partner shall not, for a period of _____ years, carry on or engage in or be interested in, either directly or indirectly, any other business competing with the business of the Partnership within a radius of _____ miles from the place of business of the Partnership.

Fee [Standard Fee]

(Agreement clause providing the terms of an annual fee for accounts rendered under contractual obligations.)

Company shall pay Undersigned an annual retainer fee for services required under this Agreement of .... dollars ($........). This fee shall be paid in equal quarterly [or, monthly] instalments payable on the first business day of each quarter commencing on [date].

Force Majeure

(Agreement clause providing a legal provision for "non-liability" in the event of any unforeseen and/or uncontrollable circumstances whether natural or otherwise)

Force Majeure: Undersigned shall not be liable under the provisions of this agreement for damages on account of strikes, lockouts, accidents, fires, delays in manufacturing, delays of carriers, acts of God, governmental actions, state of war or any other causes beyond the control of manufacturer whether or not similar to those enumerated.

Forecasts [Manufacturing Agreement]

(Agreement clause, which can be inserted into a manufacturing agreement, setting out the requirement for purchase estimate forecasts to be provided by customer to manufacturer)

MANUFACTURING AGREEMENT
Forecast of Purchase Quantities: (a) The Customer shall, on or before, and every thereafter, provide to the Manufacturer, (monthly / quarterly / half-yearly) forecasts for the next, which forecasts shall set out the following information: (i) purchase orders for the (number/quantity) of {products] required for delivery within the first; (ii) non-binding estimates of the Purchaser's anticipated requirements for [products] in the next (period of time); (b) It is understood that the forecasts provided by the Purchaser are estimates only, and are non-binding upon the Purchaser, and may be updated or amended by the Purchaser at any time and from time to time.

Freedom of Action

(Agreement clause, by which the parties agree not to limit each other's right to deal with other parties for the same services or products.)

Freedom of Action: This agreement shall not be construed to limit the Buyer's right to obtain services or software programs from other sources, to prohibit or restrict the Buyer from independently developing or acquiring competitive materials, to restrict the Buyer from making, having made, using, leasing, licensing, selling or otherwise disposing of any Products or services whatsoever, and shall not be construed to limit either party's right to deal with any other vendors, suppliers, sellers or customers.

General Disclaimer

THE UNDERSIGNED DISCLAIMS ANY AND ALL PROMISES, REPRESENTATIONS, AND WARRANTIES, EXCEPT FORTH IN THIS AGREEMENT, WITH RESPECT TO THE [DESCRIBE] OR ANY OTHER MATERIAL FURNISHED HEREUNDER, OR ANY COMPONENT THEREOF, INCLUDING THE CONDITION, THE CONFORMITY TO ANY REPRESENTATION OR DESCRIPTION, THE EXISTENCE OF ANY LATENT OR PATENT DEFECTS, AND THE MERCHANTABILITY OR FITNESS FOR A PARTICULAR USE THEREFOR.

General Provisions

(Miscellaneous clause which can be inserted into most types of contracts includes notice provisions, governing law, severability of articles and clauses, counterpart execution, interpretation, enurement (inurement), force majeure, arbitration and other general provisions.)

GENERAL LEGAL CLAUSES: Amendments. This Agreement may not be modified or amended except with the written consent of the parties.

Articles Severable: If any Article, Section, paragraph or provision of this Agreement is determined to be void or unenforceable in whole or in part, it shall not affect or impair the validity or enforcement of any other provision of this Agreement.

Contra Proferentum: This Agreement is to be deemed to have been prepared jointly by the parties here to and any uncertainty or ambiguity existing herein, if any, shall not be interpreted against any party, but shall be interpreted according to the application of the rules of interpretation for arm's length agreements.

General Release

(Agreement clause providing a general release of liability extending to heirs, assigns, executors, and administrators.)

The undersigned, in consideration of one dollar ($1.00) does hereby remise, release, and forever discharge [Name], his heirs, assigns, executors, and administrators from all actions, causes of action, claims and demands whatsoever, whether or not well founded in fact or in law, and from all suits, debts, dues, sums of money, accounts, reckonings, notes (or bonds), bills, specialties, covenants, contracts, controversies, agreements, promises, trespasses, damages, judgments, executions, claims and demands whatsoever, at law or in equity that undersigned ever had, now has, or that his heirs, executors or administrators hereafter may have against the party hereby released by reason of any matter, cause or thing whatsoever up to and including the date of this release.

[Optional]

It is the specific intent and purpose of this instrument to release and discharge any and all claims and causes of action of any kind or nature whatsoever, whether known or unknown and whether specifically mentioned or not, which may exist or might be claimed to exist at or prior to the date of this instrument and undersigned specifically waives any claim or right to assert that any cause of action or alleged cause of action or claim or demand has been, through oversight or error or intentionally or unintentionally, omitted from this release.

Governing Law

(Agreement clause stating the jurisdiction and State the agreement will be interpreted in.)

This Agreement shall be interpreted in accordance with the laws of the State of [state].

Hold Harmless

(Agreement clause providing a party harmless against any circumstances which may arise beyond reasonable circumstances)

Hold Harmless: [Name] will hold [Undersigned] harmless against any circumstances which may arise beyond [Undersigned] control [state possible circumstances]. [Name] does not hold [Undersigned] responsible for payment of taxes on wages paid to [Undersigned] during the term of this agreement or any claims for compensation. [Name] will provide adequate insurances in relation to the [Describe] and protection of said [goods/property] while under the care of [Undersigned]

Identification of Parties [Real Estate Contract]

(Agreement clause providing identification of Parties to an agreement)

Identification of Parties: [Name] (Owner) and [name] (Purchaser) have entered into [agreement] for sale of the premises located at [address] (Property). (Owner) has procured [name] (Purchaser) as a purchaser for the Property. Owner and Purchaser have executed a legal contract of sale of the Property dated [date].

Inducement [Affidavit of Title]

(Agreement clause in "Affidavit of Title" providing inducement to buy/sell/transfer of "all rights and ownership" in personal property)

I make this affidavit of title for the sole purpose of inducing [name] to accept [Summarise] described in the annexed exhibit marked "A" knowing full well that [name] will rely upon the representations made herein.

Indemnification [Partnership Agreement]

(Agreement clause providing indemnity of the other partner involved in a 50/50% general partnership.)

Each Partner shall indemnify and hold harmless the partnership and each of the other Partners from any and all expense and liability resulting from or arising out of any negligence or misconduct on his part to the extent that the amount exceeds the applicable insurance carried by the partnership.

Independent Contractor

(Agreement clause which can be inserted into any legal agreement, which provides that the relationship between the parties is to be deemed as independent contractors, not partnership, employment or agency)

Independent Contractor: The relationship between the parties hereto is intended to be, and is to be construed as, that of independent contracting parties only and not that of employment, partnership, joint venture, agency or any other association whatsoever. Nothing whatsoever contained herein shall constitute either party as having authority to bind the other in any manner whatsoever and nothing whatsoever contained herein shall give or is intended to give any rights of any kind to any third party.

Inside Information Securities Laws Violations

(Agreement clause providing inside information within the meaning and intent of the federal securities laws, rules, and regulations.)

Inside Information--Securities Laws Violations: In the course of the performance of Consultant's duties, it is expected that Consultant will receive information that is considered material inside information within the meaning and intent of the federal securities laws, rules, and regulations. Consultant will not disclose this information directly or indirectly for Consultant or as a basis for advice to any other party concerning any decision to buy, sell, or otherwise deal in Client's securities or those of any of Client's affiliated companies.

[Optional Paragraph]

Warranty That Agreement Does Not Contemplate Corrupt Practices--Domestic or Foreign. Consultant represents and warrants that (a) all payments under this Agreement constitute compensation for services performed and (b) this Agreement and all payments, and the use of the payments by Consultant, do not and shall not constitute an offer, payment, or promise, or authorisation of payment of any money or gift to an official or political party of, or candidate for political office in, any jurisdiction within or outside of the United States of America. These payments may not be used to influence any act or decision of an official, party, or candidate in his, her, or its official capacity, or to induce such official, party, or candidate to use his, her, or its influence with a government to affect or influence any act or decision of such government to assist Client in obtaining, retaining, or directing business to Client or any person or other corporate entity. As used in this Paragraph, the term "official" means any officer or employee of a government, or any person acting in an official capacity for or on behalf of any government; the term "government" includes any department, agency, or instrumentality of a government.

Issues

(Agreement clause providing an avenue for mediation of unresolved claims and disputes)

Issues: Any and all claims and disputes between the parties arising out of or relating to [Describe] or any transactions undertaken on behalf of [Name] or relative to this Agreement shall be submitted to arbitration in accordance with this Paragraph ---------

Instalment Payments

(Agreement clause clearly outlining the agreed terms of payment(s))

The Company shall pay the Undersigned the sum of ---- ------ dollars ($---------) in instalments in accordance with the payment schedule set forth in Exhibit C, and each instalments shall be payable upon completion/sale of [Describe] by the Undersigned and acceptance by the Company.

Intellectual Property Rights [Manufacturing]

(Agreement clause which can be inserted into a manufacturing agreement, setting out rights to and ownership of intellectual property, indemnification by one party of another against any claim for infringement, warranty of non-infringing design.)

MANUFACTURING AGREEMENT

Intellectual Property: Nothing contained in this Agreement shall be construed as transferring to the Customer any right, title or interest in or to any patent, industrial design, trade mark, copyright, proprietary information, design, process, method, technique, procedure or know-how (the "Intellectual Property") which is owned by the Manufacturer or its affiliates. The Manufacturer shall retain all rights to Intellectual Property relating to the [products]. Nothing herein contained shall be construed as conferring upon the Manufacturer the right to use the trademarks, trade names, logos or other business marks of the Customer in any manner whatsoever without the prior written consent of the Customer.

Life Insurance [Partnership Agreement]

(Agreement clause which can be inserted into a partnership agreement, providing that the partners can carry life insurance policies on the other partners for the amount of their respective interests.)

Life Insurance (a) The Partners agree to insure each other in an amount equal to the value of each Partner's interest in the Partnership as calculated by the valuation formula set out in paragraph _____ herein.

Limitation of Action

(Setting the limitation period for actions to be brought with respect to non-performance or non-payment)

Limitation of Actions: No action arising out of or pursuant to this Agreement may be brought by either party more than ___ years after the cause of action has arisen or, in the case of non-payment, more than _____ years from the date of the last payment.

Limitation of Liability - Manufacturing Contract

(Agreement clause which can be inserted into a manufacturing agreement, limiting the liability of Manufacturer to Customer)

Conditions for Sale (Purchase Order):
1. Purchaser reserves the right to cancel purchase if [products] not delivered within the time specified by the Vendor. In the event that shipment will be delayed, Vendor must give written notice to the Purchaser setting out the cause and anticipated duration of the delay. If the delay is in excess of _____, Purchaser may cancel this purchase order. Except in circumstances where the delay was beyond the reasonable control of the Vendor, Purchaser may charge the Vendor with any losses incurred which are attributable to such delay.

Mail Addressed to Seller

(Agreement clause providing a Buyer the right to examine and forward mail addressed to the seller.)

Mail Addressed to Seller: Following the closing, Buyer may open all mail addressed to the Seller at his or her business premises. Buyer shall properly forward to Seller any mail that does not require Buyer's action.

Minimum and Maximum Consulting Hours

(Agreement clause specifying minimum and maximum consulting hours between client and consultant)

Minimum and Maximum Consulting Hours. Consultant will furnish Client with a maximum of [number] days during the term of this Agreement, but no more than [number] days in any one calendar month. Additional time may be mutually agreed upon. Client will require a minimum of [number] days during the term of this Agreement. If, at the end of the term of this Agreement, Client has not called upon Consultant for the minimum number of days guaranteed, Client, nevertheless, will pay Consultant for the days guaranteed but not used by Client.

Mutual Release

(Clause allowing for a mutual release of parties under contractual obligations)

Each of the parties releases and discharges the other together with such party's heirs, executors, administrators, and assigns of and from all claims, clauses of action, debts, duties, liabilities, and obligations of any and every sort or nature, wherever and however arising, which against the other he now has or ever had or which he or his heirs, executors, administrators, or assigns hereafter may or can have, from any time up to and including the date of this Agreement.

No Commitment [Manufacturing Agreement]

(Agreement clause which can be inserted into a manufacturing agreement, stating that the contract is not to be construed as a commitment or obligation by Customer to purchase any product from Supplier)

MANUFACTURING AGREEMENT

Agreement not to be construed as Commitment: This Agreement is not to be construed as a commitment or obligation, express or implied on the part of the Customer that it will purchase any services or [products] under this Agreement. A signed purchase order, delivered by the Customer to the Manufacturer, shall be the only document which shall be construed as a commitment and obligation on the part of the Customer to purchase services and/or [products] hereunder, and only to the extent of such purchase order.

No Prior Agreements

(Agreement clause which can be inserted into an agreement whereby the parties acknowledge that they have not entered into any agreement)

Except as expressly provided here, the parties acknowledge that they have not entered into any agreement, understanding, whether express, implied in fact, or implied in law, on their respective property and contractual rights and obligations. The parties want to define their assignment of rights regarding their respective property, and the parties intend that this

Agreement evidence their mutual agreement on their respective property and contract rights and obligations.

No Subordination Clause--Mortgages.

(Agreement clause for additional provisions in a commercial property lease agreement.)

This Lease will not be subject or subordinate to any mortgage, unless Landlord obtains from the holder of such mortgage an agreement that as long as Tenant is not in default under this Lease, Tenant's possession will not be disturbed by any action to foreclose such mortgage or any sale on foreclosure. An executed counterpart of such agreement must be delivered to Tenant.

No Subordination Clause--Ground Leases.

(Clause for additional provisions in a commercial property lease agreement.)

This Lease will not be subject or subordinate to any underlying lease, unless Landlord obtains from Lessor under any such lease an agreement that as long as Tenant is not in default under this Lease, Tenant's Lease and possession will not be disturbed by the termination of such underlying Lease. An executed counterpart of such agreement(s) must be delivered to Tenant.

No Suits, Judgments, or Bankruptcy or Insolvency Proceedings.

(Clause which can be inserted into an agreement outlining that no actions or proceedings that would affect this agreement)

No actions or proceedings that would affect this agreement are pending in any court or other forum. There are no judgments, executions, attachments, or replevins outstanding against the Transferor. The Transferor has filed no petition in bankruptcy or for an arrangement with creditors nor has any such petition been filed against Transferor in the past [number] years. The Transferor has not taken advantage of any law relating to insolvency in the past [number] years.

Non-Competition

(Non-competition clause which can be inserted into an agreement, containing a covenant on the part of one party not to compete in the same or a similar business for the term of agreement and for a specified period.)

Non-Competition: In consideration of the terms hereof and other good and valuable consideration, the receipt and sufficiency of all of which is acknowledged by each of the parties hereto, agrees with the Company that during the period in which this Agreement is in force and during the period of five (5) years from the expiry of this Agreement, regardless of the reason for which this legal Agreement expires including (if such should be the case) unilateral breach (or repeated breach) or termination of _, neither o nor any of his Affiliates shall without the consent of the board of directors of the Company, which may be withheld or given in its sole, absolute and unfettered discretion (that need not be exercised reasonably), within _____:

(a) become employed by, engage, be or become connected, directly or indirectly through share ownership or otherwise, in any business which directly or indirectly competes with any services performed or products supplied in the conduct of the Business, or [Describe].

Non-Disclosure

(Clause which can be inserted into an agreement, by which one party agrees not to disclose confidential and proprietary information provided by other parties pursuant to the Agreement)

Non-Disclosure: _____ [name] acknowledges that sensitive and confidential information concerning the nature of the Business and activities of the Corporation may be made available to him and he agrees that he shall, and shall cause his Affiliates and any nominees of the board of directors of the Corporation to, keep confidential any information of any kind related to the business including, without limitation, the contents of any and all agreements, subscription lists, customer lists, newspaper morgues, photo files, advertising materials, contract quotations, charity contracts, documents, computer programs, tapes, books, records, files and tax returns (collectively hereinafter referred to as "Information") acquired by him while employed by the Corporation in respect of the Business or activities of the Corporation except and to the extent only that (i) such information is available to the public generally in the form disclosed, or (ii) such parties are required by law to disclose, file or register the same, or (iii) such disclosure is necessary or advisable to obtain any consent, authorization, approval or license of or from any governmental, public or regulatory body or authority on behalf of the Corporation and disclosure would not breach his duties to the Corporation or customers or clients of the Corporation or their respective Affiliates, or (iv) the Corporation has consented to such disclosure being made, or (v) such disclosure is made to professional advisors to obtain advice thereon or in connection therewith on behalf of the Corporation and such advisors are bound to keep such information confidential or (vi) disclosure is made in connection with legal proceedings on behalf of the Corporation. The parties hereto agree not to disclose any confidential information to each other with respect to this Agreement. If it becomes necessary to make such disclosure, the parties shall enter into a separate confidentiality agreement prior to making disclosure.

OR

Nondisclosure: The Undersigned will keep strictly confidential all Confidential Information and will not, without the Company's express written authorisation, signed by one of the Company's authorised officers, use or sell, market or disclose any crucial "Confidential Information" to any third person, firm, corporation or association for any purpose whatsoever. The Undersigned further agrees that the Undersigned will not make any copies of the Confidential Information except upon the Company's written authorisation, signed by one of the Company's authorized officers, and will not remove any copy or sample of "Confidential Information" from the premises of the Company without such authorisation.

Non Performance

(Agreement clause stating that a waiver of a party's rights on non-performance on the part of another party will not constitute a continuing waiver)

Non-Performance: Waiver by _____ of any provision of this Agreement in any one instance shall not constitute a waiver as to any other instance and such waiver shall be in writing. The failure on the part of any party hereto to exercise any right conferred upon it pursuant to this Agreement shall not be deemed to be a waiver of any such right or operate to bar the exercise thereof at any time thereafter.

Non Waiver

(Agreement clause providing strict performance of any provision of a signed agreement)

Non Waiver: The failure or refusal by [Name] either to insist on the strict performance of any provision of this agreement or to exercise any right in any one or more instances or circumstances shall not be construed as a waiver or relinquishment of such provision or right, nor shall such failure or refusal be deemed a custom of practice contrary to such provision or right.

Notices [General]

(Agreement clause stating the terms and conditions for notices)

Notices: All notices under this Agreement shall be in writing, sent by certified mail, postage prepaid, to the address stated in Paragraph [--] or such other address as either party may designate by prior written notice to the other.

Notices [Partnership Agreement]

(Agreement clause outlining the provision for written notice of changes by the parties involved in a 50/50% partnership.)

Notices: Any written notice to any of the Partners required or permitted under this agreement shall be deemed to have been duly given on the second day after mailing if mailed to the party to whom notice is to be given, by next-day post with certified return receipt requested, postage prepaid, and addressed to the addressee at the address stated opposite his name below, or at the most recent address, specified by written notice, given to the sender by the addressee under this provision. Notices to the partnership shall be similarly given, and address to it at its principal place of business.

Oral Changes

(Clause stating the terms and conditions for notices)

This Agreement may not be changed or terminated orally. The Agreement applies to and binds the heirs, executors, administrators, and assigns of the parties.

Ownership of Assets [Partnership Agreement]

(Clauses which can be inserted into a partnership agreement, setting out the ownership of the assets, whether by the partnership or by individual partners)

Partnership Assets Owned by Partnership: The Partners agree that all assets listed in Schedule "A" attached hereto are assets of the Partnership and that title to such assets shall be vested in the Partnership immediately on execution of this Agreement. The Partners further agree that as of the date hereof, these assets are valued at $_____. The Partners further agree that none of these assets shall be used for any purposes other than in connection with the business of the Partnership.

OR

Partnership Assets Owned by Partners: The Partners agree that all assets listed in Schedule "A" attached hereto under the names of the Partners are assets of the Partnership, but that title to each asset shall remain vested with the Partner whose name appears as Owner opposite each asset. All costs for insurance, upkeep and replacement of the assets shall be paid out of the general revenues of the Partnership.

Payment of Costs

(Agreement clause which can be inserted into an agreement setting out which party is responsible for payment of costs related to preparation of the agreement and ancillary documents.)

Costs _____ shall pay all costs, charges and expenses of and incidental to the preparation of this Agreement.

OR

Each party shall pay his own costs and expenses of and incidental to the preparation of this Agreement.

OR

The _____ agrees to pay all costs and expenses (including legal fees on an attorney and his own client basis) of _____ incurred with respect to any proceedings taken for the purpose of enforcing the rights and remedies of _____.

Payment of Invoices [Manufacturing Agreement]

(Agreement cause which can be inserted into a manufacturing agreement, setting out terms of payment of invoices for product delivered to customer, payment of taxes by customer, manufacturer retains security interest until full payment.)

MANUFACTURING AGREEMENT

Payment: The Manufacturer shall invoice the Purchaser on a _ (weekly/monthly/ bimonthly) basis. All invoices shall be net _ days. If payment is received by the Manufacturer within _____ days of the invoice date, a discount of _% will be applied. The Manufacturer may at any time, upon _ days' notice to the Customer, modify the terms of payment hereunder if, in the opinion of the Manufacturer, the financial situation of the Purchaser warrants such modification.

The Customer shall be responsible for payment of all taxes levied against the Products or under this Agreement including, without limitation, goods and services tax, sales tax, usage taxes and taxes based on gross revenues. The Manufacturer shall retain a security interest in the Products until the full purchase price there for has been paid by the Customer. The Manufacturer shall have the right to register such security interest in the applicable _____Registry to evidence such security interest. The Customer hereby appoints the Manufacturer as its attorney to execute all documents and do all things required in order to affect such registration and protect the Manufacturer's interest.

Performance of Other Party's Obligations

(Agreement clauses providing that a party to an agreement may perform the obligations of another party upon failure of the other party to do so.)

Performance of Other Party's Obligations: If either party shall fail, for any reason, to perform any provision of this Agreement to be performed by it, the other party may, at its option, perform that provision and upon doing so shall be reimbursed upon demand for all sums paid or incurred in performing that provision and shall be paid such reasonable fee for performing the provision as would be charged by an independent third party.

Purpose of Separation

(Agreement clause providing separation due to unresolved difficulties and/or non-communication either oral or written)

Purpose of Separation: [Name] and [name] agree to separate in order to resolve various (marital/business partnership) difficulties. This separation is to be temporary in nature so that the parties may determine whether or not to permanently dissolve their (marital/business partnership).

Prerequisite to Commission

(Agreement clause stating the terms and conditions of payment of commission)

Prerequisite to Commission: [Name] shall not be entitled to a commission or any other sum from [Name] unless and until title to the Property shall be transferred from [Name] to [Name]. If title does not close for any reason, other than [Name] wilful default, [Name] shall not be entitled to a commission or any other sums from Owner.

Professional Obligations

(Agreement clause stating clear and precise obligations of one or more parties to the agreement)

Professional Obligations: Undersigned shall perform all services under this Agreement in accordance with generally accepted accounting practices and principles. This Agreement is subject to the laws, rules, and regulations governing the [profession] imposed by governmental authorities or professional associations of which Undersigned is a member.

Purchase Price

(Agreement clause outlining the purchase price for goods and/or property)

Purchase Price. The purchase price is ----------- dollars ($----------), Payable in full upon delivery of [Describe], by cashier's check drawn upon a local bank.

Quality Control [Manufacturing Agreement]

(Clause in a manufacturing agreement, setting out quality control procedures and right to inspection by customer of manufacturer's procedures)

MANUFACTURING AGREEMENT

Quality Control Clauses: The Manufacturer agrees to manufacture and pack the [products] in all respects in a manner which meets the Customer's specifications. If any quantity of the [products] is found not to meet the Customer's specifications, the Manufacturer shall replace the same with [products], which meet the specifications, at the Manufacturer's expense. In the event that the Manufacturer and the Customer do not agree on whether the [brand products] meet the Customer's specifications, the [products] in question or a sufficient sample of the same shall be submitted for testing to an independent testing laboratory which has been mutually agreed upon by both parties. The determination of such independent testing laboratory shall be final and binding on both parties. The costs for such testing and determination shall be borne (a) by the Customer if the [products] are found to meet the specifications, or (b), by the Manufacturer if the [products] are found to be deficient in meeting the specifications. The Manufacturer shall permit the Customer or its duly authorised agent, upon reasonable notice, to observe the Manufacturer's quality evaluation and control procedures, and to inspect [products] prior to shipment in order to verify that such [products] conform to the Customer's specifications.

Reimbursement of Expenses

(Agreement clause providing written terms and conditions for the reimbursement of expenses)

Reimbursement of Expenses: In addition to the fee provided in Paragraph [--], Company shall reimburse Undersigned for all expenses incurred by Undersigned that are attributable or properly allowable to the services provided to Company under this Agreement. This includes travel expenses and [any major item of expected expense parties have agreed upon, e.g., meals and lodging]. In no event, however, shall Company's obligations under this Paragraph [--] exceed ……….. dollars ($......) per year unless Company agrees in writing to such further reimbursement. Undersigned's expenses shall be paid within [number] days of Undersigned's submission of a bill to Corporation accompanied by copies of vouchers or an itemized account of expenditures, but not more often than once per month.

Remedies

(Agreement clause regarding the rights and remedies under law of the parties, that the same are cumulative, may be exercised at any time. Omission of exercising right not to operate as waiver)

Remedies: Upon default by _____ to perform any obligation or satisfy any provision of this Agreement, _____ shall have all rights and remedies provided by law and by this Agreement. No delay or omission by _____ in exercising any right or remedy shall operate as a waiver of such right or remedy or of any other right or remedy under this Agreement or at law, and no single or partial exercise of a right or remedy shall preclude any other or further exercise of them or the exercise of any other right or remedy. All rights and remedies of _____ granted under this Agreement are cumulative and may be exercised at any time and from time to time independently or in combination.

Restrictive Covenant Assignable by Buyer

(Agreement clause stating Seller will remain bound by the terms of the restrictive covenant enforced by Buyer's assigns, successors, and transferees.)

Restrictive Covenant Assignable by Buyer: The restrictive covenant contained in Paragraph [--] shall inure to the benefit of Buyer's assigns, successors, and transferees. If Buyer sells or otherwise transfers the business, Seller will remain bound by the terms of the restrictive covenant that may be enforced by Buyer's assigns, successors, and transferees.

Retention and Description of Services

(Agreement providing Retention and Description of Services for consulting services)

Retention and Description of Services: During the term of this Agreement, Consultant will furnish consulting services and advice as specifically requested by [name], Client and/or Client's representative. The services and advice will relate to work being done or planned by Client in the field of [description], will be within the area of Consultant's technical competence, and will specifically include the following: [list].

Return Documents

(Agreement clause providing the way of return of Company samples and "Confidential Information")

Return Documents: Upon receipt of a written request from Company, the Undersigned will return to the Company all copies or samples of Confidential Information which, at the time of the receipt of the notice, are in the Promisor's possession.

Right to Terminate

(Agreement clause providing the right to terminate the contractual arrangement under specific terms)

Right to Terminate: Company may at any time terminate this Agreement, without cause, upon [number] days' prior written notice to Undersigned.

Right to Use Name [Partnership Agreement]

(Clause which can be inserted into a partnership agreement, providing that the remaining partners have the right to retain the name of the partnership upon the departure of a partner)

Right to Use Withdrawing Partners Name: The Partner each agree with one another that in the event of the withdrawal of any of them from the Partnership, the remaining Partners shall have the right to continue to use the name of the Partnership without compensation other than any payments made to such withdrawing Partner on account of goodwill, including the name of such withdrawing Partner.

Risk of Loss or Destruction [Sale Agreement]

(Agreement clause providing the Buying legal protection up to the closing of sale)

Risk of Loss or Destruction: Seller assumes all risk of loss or damage caused by fire, wind, or other casualty up to the closing. If the business is terminated or interrupted before the closing by loss or damage caused by fire, wind, or other casualty, Buyer may terminate this Agreement and demand the return of any sums Buyer may have paid to Seller or Seller's agent on account of the purchase price. Upon return of those sums, this Agreement shall terminate and be of no effect, and neither Buyer nor Seller shall have any further rights against each other. If the loss or damage is not sufficiently severe to terminate or interrupt the business, the purchase price shall be adjusted to reflect the loss or damage in accordance with Paragraph [--]

Rules and Regulations [Commercial Lease]

(Clause for additional provisions in a commercial property lease agreement.)

Tenant shall comply with the rules and regulations that are set out at the end of this Lease and such other rules and regulations as Landlord may reasonably formulate and give Tenant notice of during the term of this Lease.

Security Deposit [Residential Lease]

(Residential lease clause re: security deposit not to be applied as rent; landlord authorised to deliver entire security deposit to one tenant as agent for several tenants.)

Security Deposit: The Tenants shall pay the Landlord a security deposit equal to $[deposit]. The security deposit shall be held by the Landlord as security for payment of all rent and other amounts due from the Tenants to the Landlord, for the performance of the Tenants' obligations under this Lease, and against any damages caused to the Premises by the Tenants or their invitees or licensees to the Premises. The Tenants understand and agree that the security deposit may not at their option be applied as rent or against any other amount due from the Tenants to the Landlord and that the monthly rent will be paid each month including the last month of the lease term. Assuming all obligations of the Tenants have been paid and the Tenants are not in breach of any of the terms of this Lease, then upon expiry or termination of this Lease the security deposit shall be returned to the Tenants in accordance with applicable law. In the event all obligations of Tenants have not been paid, the security deposit will be returned to the Tenants less deductions in accordance with applicable law. Each Tenant hereby appoints each of the other Tenants as his authorised agent for purposes of accepting from the Landlord whatever portion of the security deposit may be attributable to him or her. The Tenants understand that this section authorises the Landlord to deliver the entire security deposit to a single Tenant and each Tenant agrees to hold harmless the Landlord in the event the Landlord returns the security deposit to a single Tenant.

Seller's Representations and Warranties

(Agreement clause clearly outlining the Seller's representations and warranties of a sale)

Seller's Representations and Warranties: Seller makes the following representations and warranties, which shall survive the closing of the sale: [Describe details and/or terms and conditions]

    a. Seller Is Sole Owner. Seller is the sole owner of the [Property] and has full right and power to sell and transfer it.
    b. No Caveats, Liens or Encumbrances. The [Property] is free from any security interest or other lien or encumbrance.
    c. Suits, Judgments, Etc. No judgments exist against Seller nor are there any executions,

attachments, or replevins outstanding against Seller. Seller is not a defendant or respondent in any action or proceeding. No petition in bankruptcy or for an arrangement of creditors has been filed by or against Seller.

Seller's Restrictive Covenant

(Agreement clause providing the buyer with a non-competition provision for a specified period of time)

Seller's Restrictive Covenant: For a period of [number] years from the date of closing, Seller will not, directly or indirectly, either as principal, partner, agent, manager, employee, stockholder, director, officer, or in any other capacity, engage or be interested in the conduct of a business similar to the one sold pursuant to this Agreement within a radius of [number] miles from the city in which the business being sold is located. This restrictive covenant will be included in the bill of sale to be delivered at the closing.

Severability

(Agreement clause providing severability for the entire duration and terms of the agreement)

If any term, provision, covenant, or condition of this agreement is held by a court of competent jurisdiction to be invalid, void, or unenforceable, the rest of the agreement shall remain in full force and effect and shall in no way be affected, impaired, or invalidated.

OR

Severability of Clauses: If any provision of this Agreement or its application is held to be invalid, illegal, or unenforceable in any respect, the validity, legality, or enforceability of any of the other provisions and applications therein shall not in any way be affected or impaired.

Special Damages

(Agreement clause providing that neither party is to be liable for special damages.)

Special or Consequential Damages: Notwithstanding any other provision in this Agreement or any applicable statutory provisions, neither party shall be liable to the other for special or consequential damages or damages for loss of use arising directly or indirectly from any breach of this Agreement, or from any acts or omissions of their respective employees or agents and in no event shall the liability of the parties exceed the value of this Agreement.

Successors

(Clause outlining the respective successors, assigns, and personal representatives of the parties)

This agreement shall be binding on and inure to the benefit of the respective successors, assigns, and personal representatives of the parties, except to the extent of any contrary provision in this agreement.

OR

Successors and Assigns: This Agreement is binding on the parties to it and on their heirs, executors, administrators, successors, and assigns.

Survival of Obligations

(Agreement clause regarding the obligations of the parties to survive termination of the agreement)

Obligations to Survive Termination (Non-Merger) Notwithstanding the termination of this Agreement for any cause, the obligations of _____ as to _____ as set forth in this Agreement shall survive any such termination and shall remain in force until discharged.

Termination of Agreement by Notice

(Clause providing termination of agreement by either party in written format by registered or certified mail.)

Either party may terminate this Agreement upon [number] days' notice by registered or certified mail, return receipt requested, addressed to the other party. If this Agreement is terminated by either party, Client shall only be liable for payment of consulting fees earned as a result of work actually performed prior to the effective date of the termination. [--] days-notice shall be measured from the date the notice is posted.

Terms of Arbitration

(Agreement clause stating the terms of arbitration and the means of legal recourse in accord with certain paragraphs as set forth in the agreement.)

Terms of Arbitration: All matters subject to arbitration under this Paragraph [---] shall be submitted to arbitration in accordance with the Rules of the Council of Arbitration or like organization, except as otherwise provided in this Agreement.

1. Arbitration shall be brought upon the written notice of one party to the other of a demand for arbitration, including a recitation of the claim or dispute for which arbitration is sought and a specification of the Arbitrator chosen by such party from a list of potential arbitrators prepared by the American Council of Arbitration or like organization. Arbitration shall be before a panel of three Arbitrators. Within [number] days of receipt of a demand for arbitration, the party receiving the demand must select a second Arbitrator from the said list and notify the other party of the first party's selection. Within [number] days thereafter, these two Arbitrators shall select a third Arbitrator from the said list. If they fail to select a third Arbitrator, then the third Arbitrator shall be designated by the American Council of Arbitration or like organization. If either party fails to designate an Arbitrator, then the claim or dispute shall be submitted to arbitration before a panel of three arbitrators chosen by the American Council of Arbitration or like organization.

2. Place. All matters subject to arbitration under this Agreement shall be arbitrated in [county, state].

3. Final Award. The award in the arbitration proceeding

shall be final and binding on the parties, and judgment on such award may be entered in any court having competent jurisdiction.

4. Fees and Expenses. All fees and expenses connected with the arbitration proceeding, other than counsel fees incurred by either party, if any, shall be shared equally by both parties.

[Alternative Paragraph]

4. Fees and Expenses. The Arbitrators are authorised to award either party a sum to compensate the party for the time and expense of the arbitration if they determine that arbitration was demanded without reasonable cause. In such event, the Arbitrators may also assess the costs of the arbitration proceeding against the party that demanded arbitration. In all other cases, the costs of the arbitration proceeding shall be assessed against the party against whom the arbitration award is determined, or against both parties if the determination is against both.

Trademarks, Service Marks, Signs and Logos

(Agreement clause granted the privilege to use, subject to the limitations of registered Trademarks, Service Marks, Signs and Logos.)

TRADEMARKS, SERVICE MARKS, SIGNS AND LOGOS: [Name] is hereby granted the privilege to use, subject to the limitations set forth below the trade name and trademark of Company/Individual. [Name] shall identify itself as an Authorized Agent in all advertising materials, other printed matter utilised by Agent in the conduct of its business during the term of this Agreement. Upon termination of the Agreement Agent shall immediately discontinue the use of the trademark and trade name of Company and [Name] shall immediately remove all signs and other printed material of any kind bearing the trademark or trade name of Company. Agent shall then have no further privilege to use the name of Company.

Transfer of Interest [Partnership Agreement]

(Agreement clause which can be inserted into a partnership agreement, setting out the restrictions or limitations on the transfer of a partner's interest)

Right of Withdrawing Partner to Sell or Compel Purchase. Any Partner or Partners wishing to withdraw from the Partnership, whose interest or combined interest, as the case may be, constitutes less than ____% of the interest of all Partners in the Partnership, may compel the remaining Partners to purchase their interests at the price arrived at under the valuation procedure set out herein, or may sell their interests to qualifying third parties in accordance with the terms of this Agreement.

Utility Charges [Commercial Lease Agreement]

(Agreement clause for additional provisions in a property lease)

Tenant will pay all utility charges, including, but not limited to, water, gas, electricity, sewage, and removal of waste materials used on or arising from use of the premises and will pay the same monthly or as they shall become due. Landlord represents and warrants that, at the time of commencement of this Lease, sufficient water, electricity, telephone, sewage facilities, and garbage removal will be available to Tenant for Tenant's intended use of the premises.

Valuation of Interests [Partnership Agreement]

(Clause which can be inserted into a partnership agreement, setting out the procedure for annual valuation of the partnership interests)

Valuation of Partnership Interests: The Partners shall annually, immediately after receiving the financial statements for the preceding financial year, set out in writing the value of their interests in the Partnership as of the date of the financial statements. The stipulated value shall be the basis for determining the purchase price for any Partner's interest, the adequacy of insurance on each Partner's life for the purpose of funding a purchase on death, and the purchase price on admission of a new Partner. If no valuation of Partnership interests is made for any financial year immediately preceding the purchase of an interest in the Partnership, the value of each Partner's interest shall be determined by the Partnership's accountants based on the last valuation made by the Partners and on such adjustments as are necessary to reflect any changes in the value of the Partnership interests since the last valuation, and the valuation made by the Partnership's accountants shall be binding on all the Partners.

Rescission of Contract

<u>NOTE</u>: **Write, Type or Scan** below legal document Template and add all pertinent facts & personal details.

THIS RESCISSION CONTRACT is made on [Date] by and between [Name] of [Address], hereinafter referred to as "First Party" and [Name] of [Address], hereinafter referred to as "Second Party", collectively referred to as the "Parties", hereby recite and declare the agreement of the Parties is as follows:

1. CONTRACT

1.1. The Parties entered into a contract on the ___ day of _____, 20 __, the said contract is attached to this Contract marked as Exhibit "A".

1.2. The Parties to the aforementioned contract and to this Contract of Rescission do hereby rescind that original Contract dated the ___ day of _____, 20 __.

1.3. The Parties upon the original Contract having been rescinded shall have any no further rights or duties there under.

1.4. All exhibits referred to in this Contract are incorporated herein in their entirety by such reference.

2. WAIVER OF DEFAULT

2.1. Failure of either party to insist upon performance

of any of the provisions of this Contract shall not be construed as a waiver of any subsequent default of the same or similar nature.

3. REPRESENTATION

3.1. The Parties represents and warrants that he or she has full power to enter into this Contract and that any material provided for the [Enumerate] does not infringe or violate the rights of any other person, including but not limited to copyright, and is original.

4. ACKNOWLEDGEMENT

4.1. The Parties acknowledges that this Contract has been entered into of his or her volition with full knowledge and information including tax consequences.

5. CONTRACT APPROVAL

5.1. The Parties believe the terms and conditions to be fair and reasonable under the circumstances.

6. NO COERCION

6.1. No coercion or undue influence has been used by or against either party in making this Contract.

6.2. The Parties acknowledge that no representations of any kind have been made to each party as an inducement to enter into this Contract other than the representations set forth herein.

7. SUCCESSORS AND ASSIGNS

7.1. This Contract is intended for the benefit of the parties hereto and their respective permitted successors and assigns.

8. INDEPENDENT COUNSEL

8.1. The Parties hereto represents and warrants that it has carefully read this Contract, and knows the contents herein, and that it has signed this Contract freely and voluntarily and that each party has obtained independent counsel in reviewing this document.

9. ENTIRE AGREEMENT

9.1. This Contract and the instruments referenced herein contain the entire understanding of the parties with respect to the matters covered herein and therein and, except as specifically set forth herein or therein, no party makes any representation, warranty, covenant or undertaking with respect to such matters.

10. AMENDMENT

10.1. No provision of this Contract may be waived or amended other than by an instrument in writing signed by the party to be charged with enforcement.

11. INDEMNIFICATION

11.1. The parties agree that they will not indemnify and hold each other harmless. This includes their subsidiaries, agents, officers, employees, and/or successors.

11.2. In addition, the parties to this Contract agree to assign against all (if any) claims, liabilities, damages, losses, penalties, punitive damages, expenses, and any arising reasonable legal fees and/or costs of any kind or amount that may arise.

11.3. This includes, but is not limited to, any amount that may result from the Party that is indemnified negligence or breach of this Contract, as well as its successors and assigns, occurring in accordance with the terms of this Contract; and

11.4. This section will remain in full force and effect, even if the Contract is terminated naturally or prematurely by either of the Parties.

12. SEVERABILITY

12.1 If any provision of this Contract shall be held to be invalid or unenforceable for any reason, the remaining provisions shall continue to be valid and enforceable. If a court finds that any provision of this Contract is invalid or unenforceable, but by limiting such provision it would become valid or enforceable, then such provision shall be deemed to be written, construed, and enforced as so limited.

13. AUTHORITY TO ENTER CONTRACT

13.1. Each Party warrants that the individuals who have

signed this Contract have the actual legal power, right, and authority to make this Contract and bind each respective Party.

14. SURVIVAL

14.1 The agreements and covenants set forth herein shall survive the Closing.

15. REVIEW OF CONTRACT

15.1. Each party hereto represents and warrants that it has carefully read this Contract and understands the contents hereof and that it has signed this Contract freely and voluntarily and that each party has obtained independent counsel in reviewing this document.

16. HEADINGS

16.1. The headings of this Contract are for convenience of reference only and shall not form part of, or affect the interpretation of, this Contract.

17. NO REPRESENTATION

17.1. Neither party has made any representations or promises, other than those contained in this Contract or in some further writing signed by the party making the representation or promise.

18. GOVERNING LAW

18.1 This Contract shall be enforced, governed by and

construed in accordance with the laws of the state of [State/Province] applicable to agreements made and to be performed entirely within such state, without regard to the principles of conflict of laws.

18.2. The parties hereto hereby submit to the exclusive jurisdiction of the united states federal courts located in [State/Province], with respect to any dispute arising under this contract, the agreements entered into in connection herewith or the transactions contemplated hereby or thereby. Both parties irrevocably waive the defense of an inconvenient forum to the maintenance of such suit or proceeding.

IN WITNESS WHEREOF, the parties have executed this Contract the day and year as first above written.

Signature _____

Full Name of "First Party"

Signature _____

Full Name of "Second Party"

Signature _____

Full Name of "Witness"

Address of Witness:

Use Notary Section When Required By State Law

This Section for Notary:

ACKNOWLEDGMENT OF NOTARY PUBLIC

STATE OF _____

COUNTY OF _____

SUBSCRIBED AND SWORN to before me on [DATE] before me, [NAME OF NOTARY], notary, personally appeared [NAME OF PERSON(S) INVOLVED], personally known to me (or proved to me on the basis of satisfactory evidence) to be the person(s) whose name(s) is/are subscribed to the within instrument and acknowledged to me that he/she/they executed the same in his/her/their authorized capacity(ies), and that by his/her/their signature(s) on the instrument the person(s), or the entity upon behalf of which the person(s) acted, executed the instrument.

I certify under the PENALTY OF PERJURY under the laws of the State of [State] that the foregoing paragraph is true and correct.

Witness my hand and official seal.

Signature _____

Notary

My commission expires: _____

(Official Seal)

Guidelines

Word Processing

You should scan or type the document in your favorite word processing application such as Microsoft Word, Notepad, Word Pad, etc., and use all of its features and functions.

It is best if you first place all of your thoughts down on paper. Once you are confident that specific areas and/or requirements of the arrangement are covered, you should then insert the information in a saved copy of the document under its new file name.

You should NEVER alter and save the original document in case of any errors and it requires retyping. Save the document under say the name of "the other party" (billsmith1.txt) etc, and keep the original as a backup.

Open the saved document, and add all relevant information pertaining to its intended use. Print the document, and again, save changes to the file you have made (billsmith1.txt).

You can always access the original document when it needs to be used more than once. You should only alter the document after it has been saved under a specific name or title.

INTRODUCTION

The nation remembers the loss of thousands, who died when planes hijacked by terrorists were flown into the twin towers in New York, the Pentagon, and a failed attempt to reach the White House. A lot of good people died on 9/11/2001, and the nation searched for the same answers that humankind has been dealing with for thousands of years. Why do bad things happen to good people? Or, a better question, why do bad things happen to God's people? Well, the trouble is we are all a part of a fallen humanity. This is no paradise and we cannot always find answers to the situations we face. The book of Job addresses these very questions and tries to come up with answers for God's people.

By reading Job, one chapter at a time, along with this devotional you will begin to understand that God's people are well equipped and able to go through adverse situations. You will recognize that some trials and tests are the first sign that a miracle is about to happen. You will gain strength in your daily trials by reading job, reading this devotional and by reflecting on God. By learning the truths outlined in this devotional you will be assured that GOD IS able to bless us when the world says it is impossible.

HOW TO STUDY

1. Read the entire chapter of Job that corresponds to the chapter you are reading in this devotional.

2. Pray the prayer at the end of each chapter.

3. Jot down any new insights from God.

TROUBLE HAPPENS TO US
Job Chapter 1

Verse 1: There was once a man in the land of Uz whose name was Job. That man was blameless and upright, one who feared God and turned away from evil.

The book of Job is probably the oldest book in the entire Bible and probably the first book to be written. Some have argued that Job, himself is a fictional character and that the heart of the matter is addressing the question of trouble.

Job's response is worth noting, in that first he did not deny his troubles and heartaches but he went into a period of mourning; which is the first step toward healing. Second, he himself, didn't engage in acts of sin, like getting drunk, becoming self-destructive, nor did he place blame on God and withdraw spiritually.

Satan was introduced as the author of evil and human troubles, and God was seen as a permission grantor of the acts of evil. This is why we must study the entire Bible to get a full understanding of evil and its cause, and why we must stay focused on the central question that the entire book of Job is answering and that is, will God's people remain faithful even in the most difficult and trying times in their lives? Being in the midst of a crisis is the best way to really know the answer to this theological, yet practical, question.

NOTES

_____

_____

_____

_____

_____

_____

_____